Scent From Heaven

Fragrance For the Soul

Mary Sanford

authorHOUSE®

AuthorHouse™
1663 Liberty Drive
Bloomington, IN 47403
www.authorhouse.com
Phone: 1-800-839-8640

.

First published by AuthorHouse 3/1/2011

ISBN: 978-1-4567-1695-0 (sc)
ISBN: 978-1-4567-1696-7 (e)
ISBN: 978-1-4567-1697-4 (hc)

Library of Congress Control Number: 2010919301

Printed in the United States of America

Dedicated

To The Lord Jesus Christ

Foreword

I pray these writings will bless you, make you laugh and lift your spirit.

God has given me these writings and poems at different times since 1981 when I was first saved.

In July of 2003 I sought the Lord to stir up that gift in me again, and He has been faithful to do so.

As God has led me I have written.

I pray the anointing that caused me to write these be felt as you read them.

Part of the proceeds from this book will go to Christian World Ministries, Kenya Africa,where James Misiko Walubayi is the Pastor and over seer of five churches and houses fifty six orphans and twenty two widows. Michael Sides is Founder and Bishop of Christian World Ministries Inc.

Acknowledgements

First and foremost I want to thank God for blessing me with this gift. Without Him I can do nothing.

I want to thank my husband, who so graciously allows me to pursue the things of God, he is a great man.

I thank my children who are my biggest fans and supporter anyone could ever have.

I thank my Pastors(Michael and Rhonda Sides) who has always taught to follow your dream .Through their leadership and covering has shown me who I am in God and for that, I am forever grateful. The messages that has been ministered over these twenty two years has been my greatest inspiration.

Derest Brown first stirred up the gift of poetry in me in 1981 as I heard her read the poems God had given her. Thank you Derest, you impacted my life tremendously.

Santina White,a God send(the Lord promised to send people for your life)with out her putting all this together,I would have been up a creek without a paddle.God Bless you

To my family and friends, all who pray with me and for me, my church family, and those who have spoken in to my life.

Contents

Foreword—vii
Acknowledgements—ix
Abundant Life—1
Amazing Jesus—2
A Mother Like You—3
A Purpose And A Plan—5
Awakening The Giant Within—6
Blessed Be God—7
Clarion Call—8
Desperation (Song)—9
Every body Don't Know Who Jesus Is—11
Fight The War—13
FRESH OIL—14
FOLLOWING YOU—15
Follow The Lord—16
God Will Arise—17
Happy Mothers Day (To my daughter Movetia)—18
Healing In God's Word—19
I Am A Servant—20
I Can Do It—21
I Will Not Be Jealous—23
It Is Jesus—24
I'm In Awe Of You—25
If You're Sin Sick—26
I Said I was Sorry—27
I LOVE YOU LORD—28
I Know—29
Keep Your Eye On the Prize—31
Letter to My Pastor—32
LORD I'M LEARNING—33
Love Is Like—34
Master Control—35
My Sister My Brother—37
On Bended Knee—38
Only you—39
One Two Three—41
Oh What Love—42
OH THAT I WOULD—43
Prayer—44
Prayer—46

RENEW US—47
Rise Up Woman Of God—48
Satisfy—49
SHOW ME LORD—50
Sit and Stand Strong—51
Somebody—52
Song—53
Staying Strong—54
Sunday Morning Bed—55
TAWNYA BIRTHDAY (My DAUGHTER IN LAW)—57
TEND YOUR GARDEN—58
That Same Jesus—59
The Fantastic four—60
The Master Plan—61
The One—62
The Rock—63
The Two Shall Become One—64
The Battle—65
There Is None Like You—66
There Is A Savior—68
This Is My Song—69
Vision—70
Wait—71
We Are His Sheep—72
We're Going To Rise—73
We Have The Power—74
What Plan God Has For Me—76
What Do You Want—78
What Is A Father (To My Son-In-Law)—80
Without Faith—81
WHOM THE SON SETS FREE—82
You Are the Rock—83
You Are My Source—85
You Have To Share It—86
YOUR SPIRIT—88
YOU SAY—89
A TRIBUTE TO OUR SISTER FANNIE GILES (June
1935-April 1999)—91
A Tribute To our Sister (Gladys Baker, Jan 21, 1937- Aug
15-2001)—92
Tribute To My Oldest Sister Eva Mae Wilborn—94
A BROTHER LIKE MINE—97

Abundant Life

Abundant Life

Leave it to Jesus, who won't think twice

He'll give you all you need

He'll give you abundant life

John 10:10b(KJV)

I am come that they might have life, and that they might have it more abundantly

Amazing Jesus

Amazing Jesus

How sweet is your name

You're always with us

You never change

Some trust in horses, land or fame

But I ever trust in Jesus name

Never to leave me

Never to change

Money is fleeting

It takes wings to fly

But oh sweet Jesus

You are always nearby

Psalms 9:10(KJV)

And they that know thy name will put their trust in thee: for thou, Lord has not forsaken them

that seek thee

A Mother Like You

Has Lost her own Mother

But is one for all those in her life

That's a Mother like you

Sees her children future

And points them in that direction

A Mother like you

Made mistakes and God has washed all the condemnation away

A Mother like you

Prays as she sees her children struggle through life's hurts

A Mother like you

Fights till her last breath is gone

A Mother like you leaves a legacy

For her children to follow and is never forgotten

That's a Mother like you

04/10/08

A Purpose And A Plan

A purpose and a plan

All of this is in your hand

Seek God first

For He is true

He will always see you through

Don't wait or hesitate

Don't let it be said too late

Make Godly choices

And you'll see

Why Jesus died for you and me

Don't be afraid to fail

For He is the one who took the Nails

Keep your eyes on things above

He will show you His never ending love

Jeremiah 29:11()New Living Translation

For I know the plans I have for you, says the Lord

They are plans for good and not disaster, to give you a future and a hope

10/12/04

Awakening The Giant Within

Awakening The Giant Within

It is He who will keep you from sin

The one who knows you through and through

The one who knows what to do

Which way to go, you might say

Only the Giant within knows the way

He is the truth the light

He is the one who does what's right

He is the peace in every storm

He is the one who will do you no harm

The sleeping Giant within

The one who ensures you win

1 John 4:4 (KJV)

Ye are of God, little children, and have overcome them: because greater is he that is in you, than he that is in the world.

March 28, 2010

Blessed Be God

Blessed be God who has s

Who has carried me over

Who makes my sleep s'

Blessed be God who holds me in the palm of His ha....

Who loves me in spite of myself

Blessed be God who watches over

And protects me and mine

Ephesians 1:3(KJV)

Blessed be the God and father of our Lord Jesus Christ

who has blessed us with all spiritual blessings in heavenly places in Christ;

12/07/1983

3:33pm

7

ss and Holiness is the clarion call

iis in mind lest you fall

Our God is the same yesterday and forever

He never changes, no not ever

What he says to one He says to all

Take heed to the clarion call

1PETER 1:16 (KJV)

Because it is written, Be ye holy; for I am holy.

06/22/2007

Desperation (Song)

Gotta have you near

Lord I need you near

Lord I want you near

Gotta have you near

Gotta have you near

I need you near

Gotta have you near

Lord I want you near

I need you near

Gotta have you near

Lord I need you near

Gotta have you near

I need you near

Gotta have you near

Lord I want you near

Gotta have you near

Lord I need you near

Gotta have you near

I want you near

Gotta have you near

Lord I Want you near

Gotta have you near

Lord I want you near

Gotta have you near

September 22,2009

Every body Don't Know Who Jesus Is

Everybody don't know who Jesus is

He came from Heaven to do Gods' will

He's not just a good man or someone to look up to

He came to save sinners like me and you

We should love Him with all our heart

Looking to Him never to depart

He's our Savior and there's no one like Him from above

No one desires worship or love as much as He does

He came to save us and set us free

All we have to do is follow Him and see

He's our Savior the one we should adore

He's our Savior who loves us more and more

He cleanses our sin, when we call on His name

He stands at the door waiting to come in

Everybody don't know who Jesus is

Look to Him and do His will

There are none born righteous

No not one

Jesus the begotten Son

The only one

Matthew 1:21(KJV)

And she shall bring forth a son, and thou shalt call his name JESUS: for he shall save his people from their sins.

11/12/03

Fight The War

There's a war going on in this life

The Lord did not promise we would have no strife

Fight the war without fear

For you know our God is near

He promised not to leave nor forsake

And this promise you surely need to take

There's a change in the wind

Surely the Holy Ghost He will send

You shall receive power with this great gift

To win this battle, to make it swift

Deuteronomy 31:6 (KJV)

Be strong and of a good courage, fear not, nor be afraid of them: for the LORD thy God, he it is that doth go with thee; he will not fail thee, nor forsake thee.

02/04/1999

FRESH OIL

FRESH OIL FROM HEAVEN

COMES FROM ABOVE

ALL BECAUSE OF YOUR UNSELFISH LOVE

WHICH COMES TO ALL IF WE CALL ON YOUR NAME

REALIZING YOU ARE ALWAYS THE SAME

YESTERDAY ,TODAY AND FOREVER AMEN

Psalms 92:10(KJV)

But My horn shall thou exalt like the horn of a unicorn shall be anointed with fresh oil

08/05/05

FOLLOWING YOU

Following you is the way to go

In our hearts, your love you sow

In your Word is the breath of life

Which will free us from all strife

Trust in the Lord with all your heart

Lean on him He'll never depart

(John 12:26a)[26]

If any man serve me, let him follow me;

7/25/05

Follow The Lord

Follow the Lord as the Spirit leads

Whatever He says ,be wise and take heed

Don't go before Him or stand by His side

Stay behind and follow

Lest your feet surely slide

He is a solid foundation

A tried cornerstone

Stay close to him and you'll never be alone

Romans 8:14(KJV)

For as many as are led by the Spirit of God, they are the sons of God

09/14/07

God Will Arise

In perpetual darkness God will arise

With the light of Heaven to make you wise

To lead and guide you as the day goes by

So that you will know you are the Apple of His eye

Deuteronomy 32:10

He found him in a desert land, and in the waste howling wilderness, He led him about, He instructed him, He kept him the apple of His eye

05/26/07

Happy Mothers Day (To my daughter Movetia)

Sometimes we can hardly believe we have such a brilliant and beautiful daughter as you.

You are imparting into your family the history and legacy of all the Mothers and Grandmothers that have imparted Into you.

Our prayer is that you be a greater Mother than all of us .Your children are arrows in your hands.

Continue to point them toward Jesus and their individual destines,that only a mother can see.

To coin a phrase from the younger generation

You Rock

Healing In God's Word

I will forgive

I will let live

There's healing in God's word to live

I will live

I'll give and give

I won't take away

There's healing in God' word for me

That's all I've ever heard

There's healing in God's word

Proverbs 16:24(KJV)

Pleasant words are as an honeycomb *, sweet to the soul, and health to the bones

02/24/2001

I Am A Servant

I am a servant like you told me to be

Serving others to see them set free

Whom the Son sets free is free indeed

We are the Lords' servant we supply any need

Feeding the hungry and planting a seed

staying humble is the secret to this call

Being a servant will keep you from the fall

Mark 10:44 (KJV)

And whosoever of you will be the chiefest, shall be servant of all.

09/14/07

I Can Do It

I believe I can do it

I believe I can hit the mark

I knew I could do it

Right from the very start

Not because of who I am

But because of Jesus in me

By his power I have been set free

Free to think and to dream

Believing I can do more than it seems

I have the power I have always heard

but I really didn't know it till I read His word

The word is the key that unlocks all you can be

Philppians 4:13 (KJV)

I can do all things through Christ which strengtheneth me

06/19/2007

I Will Not Be Jealous

Lord I will not be jealous when others are blessed

For if we are faithful, we will be next

You are no respecter of man

We are able to do anything if you say we can

There are no limits to what we can do

When we put our hope and trust in you

There are no limits

There is nothing bound

Keep your mind on Jesus

All these treasures will be found

Romans 2:11(KJV)

For there is no respect of persons with God

06/20/07

It Is Jesus

It is Jesus who has caused me to shine

It is Jesus who has help me tow the line

It is Jesus who has caused me to rest

It is Jesus who has given me His best

It is Jesus who has caused me to see

It is Jesus who has set me free

It is Jesus who died for me

Mark 10:27 (KJV)

And Jesus looking upon them saith, With men it is impossible, but not with God: for with God all things are possible

Nov 1,2007

I'm In Awe Of You

I'm in awe of you O Lord

Your Majesty on high

I worship and praise you

With tears of joy I cry

Psalms 33:8(KJV)

Let all the earth fear the Lord: let all the inhabitants of the world stand in awe of Him

03/06/1999

If You're Sin Sick

If you're sin sick and can't get well

Felling like you're in hell

Look to Jesus

Who's promised to save you

From all you could ever do

He'll wash you and make you clean

If on Him you will only lean

He's the great physician ,the great I AM

He'll save your soul and you won't be dammed

James 5:15(KJV)

And the prayer of faith shall save the sick

And the Lord will raise him up: and all who have committed sin Shall be forgiven

I Said I was Sorry

I said I was sorry

I've gone as far as I can

I'm only human, I'm only a man

Through many a sorrow and many a woe

Now I've come knocking at your door

I've heard you are the Savior

Who came to die for me

I've heard that you are able to set me free

Now I believe and have no doubt

That you will surely bring me out

Acts 3:19 (KJV)

Repent ye therefore, and be converted that your sins
may be blotted out ,when the times of refreshing shall
com from the presence of the Lord

I LOVE YOU LORD

I love you Lord tomorrow

I love you Lord today

I love you Lord tomorrow

And I will love you the rest of my days

I love you because you're worthy

I love you because you're true

I love you because you gave your all

I love you because you won't let me fall

I love you because you made the way

I'll love you for the rest of my day

August 23(Monday on plane)

1 John 4:19(KJV)

We love him, because he first loved us.

I Know

I know the joy of the Lord is my strength

I know weeping may endure for a night

But joy cometh in the morning

I see through a glass darkly

My deliverance is just ahead

I can't give up now

As my soul is being fed

The word of God is true

Keep it before your eyes

And see what it'll do

In it is an answer for you

Hosea 6:3a(KJV)

Then shall we know, if we follow on to know the
LORD:

08/05/03

Keep Your Eye On the Prize

Keep your eye on the prize

Don't get sidetracked

It's the plan of the enemy to set you back

Look not to the left or the right

Always keep Jesus in your sight

The enemy is waiting just to see you fall

Always make Jesus your all in all

There are many distractions coming your way

Keep your focus on Jesus each and every day

Philippians 3:14(KJV)

I press toward the mark for the prize of the high calling of Christ Jesus

Letter to My Pastor

You're doing the work a Pastor should do

Praying the prayers to see us through

GOD is not slack concerning His word

Just wait on the Lord for your prayers have been heard

The Saints of GOD pray for you each day

Knowing that GOD will show you the way

The vision you saw is already up

Now GOD will fill your cup

The spirit of poverty has been bound as you see

GOD is supplying our every need

Rest in the Lord for His promises are true

What ever you've asked He will do

1 Thessalonians 5:13(KJV)

And esteem them very highly in love for their works sake

12/17/1999

LORD I'M LEARNING

LORD I'M LEARNING HOW TO LEAN ON YOU

WITHOUT YOU I DON'T KNOW WHAT I WOULD DO

I AM HELPLESS WITHOUT YOU AS MY GUIDE

FOR WITHOUT YOU I WOULD SURELY SLIDE

WHEN I'M CAUGHT IN THE MIST OF A STORM

I TRUST IN YOU THAT I WOULD FEEL NO HARM

2 Corinthians 3:5(KJV)

Not that we are sufficient of ourselves to think any thing as of ourselves; but our sufficiency is of God;

7/27/05

Love Is Like

Love is like a fountain

That never dries up

Love is like a valley

Where the depths never end

Love is like a song

Whose melody is sweet

Love is like a river

Whose borders never bend

Love is like a gentle breeze

That blows endlessly

8/25/03

1 CORINTHIANS 13:4(Amplified)

Love endures long and is patient and kind; love never is envious nor boils over with jealousy, is not boastful or vainglorious, does not display itself haughtily.

Master Control

Have you had an overdose of backsliding today

Have you said something wrong along the way

There is an answer for those who can't cope

Take Jesus three times a day

The best antidote

Your temper is raging

And out of control

Get counseling from Jesus and take hold

Your love is growing cold

And your speech is much too bold

Why not let Jesus at your master control

Psalms 141:3(KJV) Set a watch, O Lord, before my mouth; keep the door my lips

01/19/1986

My Sister My Brother

Hello my sister, my brother ,my friend

My joy is to serve you till the end

To lift up those cast down, forelorned and in doubt

To the point of joy

To the point of a shout

Hebrews 12:12(KJV)

Wherefore lift up the hands which hang down, and the feeble knees;

01/01/1985

On Bended Knee

On bended knee I seek your face

Knowing of you and your great grace

When I look to you

You won't turn away

Listening to every word I say

Before I call

The answer's on the way

Isaiah 65:24(New Living Translation)

I will answer them before they even call to me.

While they are still talking about their needs,

I will go ahead and answer their prayers

09/12/07

Only you

Only you can answer prayer

Only you really & truly care

You give us what we need

So that we can share

It's only you that truly care

There's no one like you

To whom can I compare

It's only you who truly care

You satisfy the longing soul

Open our eyes and heart too

To allow you in to do what only you can do

1 Peter 5:7(KJV)

Casting all your care upon Him; for He careth for you

10/16/04

One Two Three

One ,two, three

I've been set free

Four, five, six

I won't get sick

Seven, eight, nine

I won't be left behind

Ten, eleven, twelve

I will live in wealth

04/04/2003

Mark 11:23(KJV)

For verily I say unto you, That whosoever shall say unto this mountain, Be thou removed, and be thou cast into the sea; and shall not doubt in his heart, but shall believe that those things which he saith shall come to pass; he shall have whatsoever he saith.

Oh What Love

Oh what love

You have bestowed upon us

Who are but merely dust

From the beginning we were on your mind

You had a plan for all man kind

A plan for our good

To die on a cross of wood

There is no greater love than this

Oh what love

John 15:13(KJV)

Greater love hath no man than this that a man **lay down his life** for **his** friends.

05/22/07

7:15am

OH THAT I WOULD

Oh that I would live for the King

Make Him my Lord and live again

Share with others as each day pass

Knowing that only what we do for Christ will last

We cannot live from day to day

Forgetting that He is the only way

We must keep our eye on the prize

Seeing it is He who keeps us alive

John 14:6(KJV)

Jesus saith unto him, I am the way ,the truth ,and the life......

10/16/04

Prayer

Prayer, prayer, prayer

A time to bathe in your glory

To meditate on the age old story

A story of the Savior

Who came on the Scene

To die on a cross

For the good and the mean

The battle has been fought

The victory has been won

Through prayer and acknowledging

The Father and the Son

John 14:13

And whatsoever ye shall ask in my name, that will I do, that the Father may be glorified in the Son

05/24/07 6:42am

Prayer

Prayer is the key

That opens Heavens' door

To Heavens' treasure forever more

When you call

He will take heed

He will supply your every need

Develop a prayer life and you will see

He has a plan for you and me

Jeremiah 29:12 (KJV)

Then shall ye call upon me, and ye shall go and pray unto me, and I will hearken unto you.

5/12/07

RENEW US

Renew us day by day

Keep us in your perfect way

The way of a transgressor is very hard

But you made a way from the very start

By touching our mind and our heart

Renew us with your perfect touch

For we need you, very much

Renew our mind and our soul

With your Word, we must take hold

Romans 12:2 (KJV)and be not conformed to this world: but be ye transformed by the renewing of your mind

7/02/05

Rise Up Woman Of God

Rise up woman of God, be all that you can be

For Jesus of Nazareth has set you free

Don't look to the left or to the right

Keep Jesus your Savior always in your sight

Don't compare yourself to those near or far

Just be like Jesus and who you are

You're a queen and princess because of Gods' love

Which He sent for you from up above

Woman of God don't despair

For your Savior Jesus really does care

Woman of God don't settle for less

When God has for you the very best

In yourself, you need to take pride

Laying all condemnation aside

Jesus did not come to condemn

But that you may be saved through Him

Take your rightful place and stand tall

For Jesus your Savior paid the price for all

September 2004

Satisfy

Only you can satisfy the hungry soul

Only you can make me whole

Only you can fill the emptiness

Only you can give me the best of the best

Isaiah 58:11(KJV)

And the LORD shall guide thee continually, and satisfy thy soul in drought, and make fat thy bones: and thou shalt be like a watered garden, and like a spring of water, whose waters fail not.

05/22/2008

SHOW ME LORD

Show me Lord which way to go

Show me Lord and I won't say no

Show me the vision and the plan

You Lord have it in your hand

Show me Lord for you can see

All that you have for me

Psalms 25:4 (KJV)

Show me thy way s O Lord: teach me thy paths

8/07/05

Sit and Stand Strong

Sit and stand strong

Realize you can't do it on your own

It's Jesus who gives you the power

Every minute, every hour

He's the great master builder

On Him you must lean

Trusting and believing

Even though He can't be seen

Ephesians 6:10(KJV)

Finally my brethren, be strong in the Lord, and the power of His might

Somebody

It's good to have somebody on your side
Who can protect you from the tide

Not just anybody

But somebody who will see you through
Who just won't let you make do

Somebody who'll be your friend
Somebody who will be with you till the end

Not just anybody will do

It's Jesus Christ of Nazareth, who you need
To your soul He will feed

Not just anybody will do
It's Jesus Christ who will be with you

Hebrews 13:5b(KJV)

For He hath said I will never leave thee nor forsake thee

Song

Each time He calls your name

you hearken to His voice

Each time your thoughts meets His

You rest in his sweet peace

Each time He sends a breeze

You feel His loving touch

Each time is the best time of your life

Just to know that you are there means all the world to me

Just to know you always care makes each new day so free

10/06/03

Staying Strong

Thank you for staying strong

Always know you are not alone

Your faith in God has carried you through

Never forget His love for you

To Him, take all your care

For He will always be there

Ephesians 6:10(KJV)

Finally my brethren, be strong in the Lord, and in the power of His might

06/2003

Sunday Morning Bed

On Sunday morning the bed feels soo good
And in it to stay you wish you could

But during the week you press your way
But on Sunday morning your body says no way

The mattress seems to sing a song
"Stay in bed where you belong"

Then your spirit begins to say "get up"
This is the Lord's Day

Your body wants to put you on hold
but your spirit shouts," I'm in control"

Get up! Sing and pray
To the Lord's house I'm on my way

There is a word for me in the house of the Lord
To miss it, I can't afford

The bed feels nice

As nice as can be

But there's a word at church that'll set me free

So don't be fooled when your bed starts to sing

"Stay here in bed with me, sweet rest I will bring

1Corinthians9:27(Message Bible)

I am staying alert and in top condition. I'm not going to get caught napping, telling everyone else all about it and then missing out myself.

2/12/1999

TAWNYA BIRTHDAY (My DAUGHTER IN LAW)

May God bless and keep you in His ever loving care

May God take you where you would never dare

May God guide you each and every day

May God keep you in His perfect way

April 06 2008

TEND YOUR GARDEN

TEND YOUR GARDEN THAT'S WHAT YOU'VE SAID

GIVE US THIS DAY OUR DAILY BREAD

IN YOU I TRUST AND WILL BE FED

BY YOU I SHALL BE LED

YOUR WORD IS AN ETERNAL SEED

IN IT IS FOUND ALL THAT WE NEED

Genesis 2:15(KJV)

And the **LORD God took** the **man,** and put **him** into the **garden** of **Eden** to **dress** it and to **keep** it.

7/27/05

That Same Jesus

That same Jesus
Who came form Galilee

That same Jesus who died for you and me
That same Jesus who walked upon the sea
That same Jesus will set you free

That same Jesus who died upon the cross
That same Jesus who died for us all

That same Jesus who loved us till the end
That same Jesus is now my friend

That same Jesus who was tortured sore
That same Jesus will suffer no more

That same Jesus who died upon a tree
That same Jesus is coming back for you and me

Hebrews 13:8(KJV)
Jesus the same yesterday, and today, and forever

The Fantastic four

With these on your side we can open any door

Father, Son, Holy Ghost, and you

Moving forward there's nothing you can't do

In order to walk in this awesome power

We have to seek Him every hour

It's not about me

We have to cooperate with the three

1 John 5:7 (KJV)

For there are three that bear record in heaven, the Father, the Word, and the Holy Ghost: and these three are one.

10/12/07

8am

The Master Plan

The Masters plan is in your hand

On it you will surely stand

It is a gift sent from above

From your Heavenly Father, who is filled with love

He sent His only begotten Son

To Him He says' well done

GOD sent His son with a plan

To die on the cross for every man

The sky is the limit

So don't despair

For God has shown how much He care

You have the freedom to choose

Choose the right path and you won't lose

Proverbs 2:6 (KJV)

For the LORD giveth wisdom: out of his mouth cometh knowledge and understanding

10/03/2004

The One

You are the rock on which I lean

You are the one that I never even seen

You are the one who I love and fear

You are the one who is always near

You are the one, Jesus

1 John 5:20 (Contemporary English Version)

And we know that the Son of **God** is come, and hath given us an understanding, that we may know him that is **true**, and we are in him that is **true**, even in his Son Jesus Christ. This is the **true God**, and eternal life.

March 28, 2010

The Rock

You are the Rock on which we can stand
We reach to you with an out stretched hand

You are steady and will not lean
The half of your power has never been seen

You are more than we hoped for
More than we can understand
Without you we stand on sinking sand

You love us in spite of our faults
You see the intent of our heart
Yet, you and your love will never depart

Psalms 62:2(KJV)
He only is my rock and my salvation;
He is my defense. I shall not be greatly moved

10/16/04

The Two Shall Become One

Then the two shall be one

Declare this together and it shall be done

Until death do we part

You have said

By His Spirit always be led

For better or for worse

Is your vow

Look to the Savior

He'll show you how

Genesis 2:24 KJV)

Therefore shall a man leave his father and his mother, and shall cleave unto his wife: and they shall be one flesh.

04/22/08

The Battle

There's a battle going on

Between the flesh and the soul

Look to Jesus, that's what I've been told

The battle may be strong

His promises is you're never alone

Fight the good fight of faith

You'll win, if you'll only wait

To the young and the old

The half of the story has not yet been told

Romans 7:22(KJV)

For I delight in the law of God after the inward man:

23 But I see another law in my members, warring against the law of my mind, and bringing me into captivity to the law of sin which is in my members

There Is None Like You

Whom the Son sets free is free indeed

You supply our every need

Our hopes and dreams, we place in you care

For in you there is no despair

We call , you answer

That's peace beyond compare

There's none like you in this world

That can stand beside you

Or fit your shoe

There is none like you

That can do what you do

Isaiah 40:18 (KJV)

To whom then will ye **liken God?** or what **likeness** will ye **compare** unto him?

October 16/05

There Is A Savior

There is a Savior who is so near

There is a Savior Who hears your

Your faintest cry

There is a Savior who is always nearby

Call on Him while He may be found

For there will come a time

When He will not hear that sound

Isaiah 55:6(KJV)
Seek ye the Lord while He may be found
Call ye upon Him while He is near
10/09/07

This Is My Song

This is my praise

This is how I carry on

This is my heart

This is my life

And to you I give the praise

This is my song

This is my heart

This how I carry on

This is my life

This is my joy

In you I do rejoice

This is my song

This is my song

This is my song

Psalm 28:7

7The LORD is my strength and my shield; my heart trusted in him, and I am helped: therefore my heart greatly rejoiceth; and with my song will I praise him.

September29,2009

Vision

You must have a vision

You must have a plan

For on your own you cannot stand

Without a vision you will surely fail

Write it down, to the last detail

Not just a thought or just an idea

And just don't look at a career

God has a plan for you

Seek and you'll find

That you can go forward

And not stay behind

There is a place you'll be totally free

Seek the Lord and you'll see

Our Lord and Savior Has an out stretched hand

In Him you will find your greatest plan

Proverbs 29:18a(KVJ)

Where there is no vision the people perish......

10/03/04

Wait

Lord Jesus you are worth the wait

When sin comes along don't hesitate

Say yes to Jesus and no to sin

In him you know you win

There is no temptation you receive

That God won't make a way to leave

He is true and faithful, just and pure

You can count on him

For this I am sure

Psalm 27:14 (KJV)

Wait on the LORD: be of good courage ,

and he shall strengthen thine heart:

wait ,I say, on the LORD.

April 29, 2010

We Are His Sheep

We are His sheep
and hear His voice

We won't listen to a sound
that tries to keep us down

But hears the voice of the Shepherd
That never leads us astray

But under the sound of His voice
We will forever stay

JOHN 10:27 (KJV)

My sheep hear my voice, and I know them, and they
follow me:

We're Going To Rise

We're going to rise to tell

the age-old story

The story that you came as a babe

and that you died on a cross

For our sins and for all who are lost

We're going to tell of your matchless glory

We're going to sing of the love that you give

We're going to praise you as long as we live

Psalms 119:62a(KJV)
At midnight I will rise to give thanks unto thee

10/10/07

We Have The Power

We have the power

We have the choice

To live right

To lift up our voice

Not just for show or tradition of man

But to show the world we will take a stand

We do this to the praise of our savior

Who has shown us His favor

He chose us and not we Him

To God be the Glory

Forever Amen

Micah 3:8a (KJV)

But truly I am full of power by the Spirit of the Lord.......

01/01/1985

What Plan God Has For Me

What God has planned for me

I know He has one

What? I cannot see

If I ask He will reveal

If only on my knees I will kneel

He will always answer

He always does

Because of His unyielding Love

Only God who is all in all

Will be with you

Even when you fall

A good man falls seven times a day

He will rise only if he will pray

A plan, a plan I must see

What all Jesus has for me

Jeremiah 10:23(New Living Translation)

I know ,Lord ,that a person's life is not his own

No one is able to plan his own course

10/05/2004

What Do You Want

What do you want from the Lord today

Healing, Faith a word from God you say

Whatever you want

Don't despair

It's Jesus who loves you

It's Jesus who cares

Ask what you will

There's nothing too hard

The Savior who died for you will never depart

Try me ,He says

Prove me too

Then will He show His love to you

He'll pour out a Blessing

You'll not have room to receive

If you only trust Him

If you only believe

Psalms 34:9 Oh fear the Lord, ye His saints :for there is no want to them that fear Him(KJV)

01/01/1985

What Is A Father (To My Son-In-Law)

A father is not perfect

But is always there

A father shows his love by how much he care

Not only in his words but, the day to day of what he does

A father builds back up, what the world has torn down

A father accomplishes that by always being around

The great gifts

The good food

Would not mean a thing

If you're not there to share

In what it really means

Written for greeting cards

June 2008

Without Faith

Without faith we cannot please

Trust in Him and always believe

Doubt and worry will keep you out

Keep your faith strong and stout

Faith without works is dead

Keep the faith and by Him be led

Hebrews 11:6 (KJV)

But without faith it is impossible to please him:

06/11/07

WHOM THE SON SETS FREE

WHOM THE SON SETS FREE IS FREE INDEED

HE WILL SUPPLY OUR EVERY NEED

OUR HOPES AND DREAMS WE PLACE IN YOUR CARE

FOR IN YOU THERE IS NO DESPAIR

WE CALL,YOU ANSWER

THAT'S PEACE BEYOND COMPARE

THERE'S NONE LIKE YOU IN THE WHOLE WIDE WORLD

THAT CAN STAND BESIDE YOU OR FIT YOUR SHOE

THERE IS NONE THAT CAN DO WHAT YOU DO

John 8:36 (KJV)

If the Son therefore shall make you free, ye shall be free indeed

10/10/04

You Are the Rock

You are the rock that we stand on

That will never lean

The half of what you can do, has never been seen

You're more than we've hoped for

More than we can understand

When you reach out to us

You give us your hand

You love us in spite of our faults

You see the intent of our heart

Yet you and your love will never depart

1 Corinthians 10:4(KJV)

And did all drink the **same spiritual drink: for** they **drank of** that **spiritual Rock** that followed **them: and** that **Rock was Christ**

You Are My Source

I've tapped into the treasure

Who gives blessing without measure

Jesus Christ the lover of our soul

Jesus Christ who makes us whole

Colossians 2:10 (KJV)

And ye are complete in him, which is the head of all principality and power:

03/06/05

You Have To Share It

You have to share it

It's not yours anyway

Not just tomorrow

Or for one day

The Love of God That's in your heart

Of course you know it'll never depart

It's shed abroad in us

And it's free

There is always someone who has a need

To feel the love and know Jesus saves

Romans 5:5b(KJV)

Because the love of God has been shed abroad in our hearts

by the Holy Ghost which is given unto us.

YOUR SPIRIT

YOUR SPIRIT FLOW

ONLY FOR THOSE WHO TRULY KNOW

THE POWER OF YOUR LOVE

THAT YOU SENT FROM HEAVEN ABOVE

YOUR SPIRIT FLOW

MATTHEW 3:16 (KJV)

And Jesus, when he was baptized, went up straightway out of the water: and, lo, the heavens were opened unto him, and he saw the Spirit of God descending like a dove, and lighting upon him

08/05/05

YOU SAY

JESUS YOU SAY YOU ARE THE SON OF GOD

THE FATHER AGREES AND HE NODS

YOU SAY YOU SET THE CAPTIVES FREE

WHOM THE SON SETS FREE IS FREE INDEED

WHAT CAN A MAN DO WHEN YOU SAY NO

ALL HE CAN DO IS LET GO

WHEN GOD SHUTS A DOOR

NO MAN CAN OPEN

IF YOU SAY YES, MAN WILL REJOICE

WHEN GOD OPENS A DOOR

NO MAN CAN CLOSE

Matthew 5:18 (KJV)

For verily I say unto you, Till heaven and earth pass, one jot or one tittle shall in no wise pass from the law, till all be fulfilled

November 25,2005

A TRIBUTE TO OUR SISTER FANNIE GILES (June 1935-April 1999)

MAMA SAID SHE NEVER HAD TO SPANK

AS WE GREW OLDER,

SHE IS THE ONE WE HAD TO THANK

SHE WOULD GIVE WITHOUT A BLINK OF THE EYE

SHE SHOWED SHE CARED WOTHOUT GIVING IT A TRY

ALL WHO KNEW HER ALWAYS WOULD SAY

SHE WAS THE LIFE OF THE PARTY

AND COULD COOK THE BEST FOOD YOU EVER WOULD TASTE

SHE WAS A WORLD TRAVELER AND WENT TO EVERY PORT

WHEN THE LORD CALLED HER

SHE WAS READY AND GAVE HIM HER HEART

A Tribute To our Sister (Gladys Baker, Jan 21, 1937- Aug 15-2001)

A Legacy of joy, laughs and smiles is what I see when I check your file

Giving, listening and being there for all

Ready and waiting for that one call

Reaching out a hand to those in need

Not just watching the hungry but taking time to feed

Your children rise up and called you blessed, for making their home a cozy nest

Your husband, who loves with all his heart

Eager to please you from the very start

Stood by your side till the very end

Being to you the best of friend

An example to your grandchildren to see and to learn

Eager to receive your love, they didn't need to earn

A devoted wife, mother and friend

You shared your love till the very end

During your illness you did not waiver nor fane

Relying totally on Jesus name

You are now at peace

your pains and cares have ceased

And you to God we do release

We'll miss you of course

But we'll be o.k.

Knowing that you're with Jesus every single day

A brand new body and a brand new life

Into the promise you've heard all your life

On streets of glory, we'll see you there

Face to face ,so kind so fair

Thinking of the love you've shown through the years

Will ease our sorrow and dry our tears

To God be the glory for loving you so

In to His arms we release you to go

Tribute To My Oldest Sister Eva Mae Wilborn

March 1, 1939-July 1,2009

A plain and simple woman

So sweet ,so dear

Someone you always wanted to be near

A big heart, A big smile

When you were around her you'd want to stay awhile

A wise woman in her own way

She took care of her business day by day

When she knew you were sick

You could always count on her to be by your side

When you stopped by her house

You never left empty handed

Always a giver, always kind

She was the best friend you could ever find

As Proverbs 31:10-12,14-18,(Contemporary English Version) says:

[10]A truly good wife

is the most precious treasure

a man can find!

[11]Her husband depends on her,

and she never

lets him down.

12She is good to him

every day of her life,

14She is like a sailing ship

that brings food

from across the sea.

15She gets up before daylight

to prepare food

for her family

and for her servants. [a] **16**She knows how to buy land

and how to plant a vineyard,

17and she always works hard.

18She knows when to buy or sell,

and she stays busy

until late at night.

20and she helps the poor

and the needy.

25She is strong and graceful, [b] as well as cheerful

about the future.

26Her words are sensible,

and her advice

is thoughtful.

27She takes good care

of her family

and is never lazy.

28Her children praise her,

and with great pride

her husband says,

29"There are many good women,

but you are the best!"

30Charm can be deceiving,

and beauty fades away,

but a woman

who honors the LORD

deserves to be praised.

31Show her respect--

praise her in public

for what she has done.

SHE FOUGHT A GOOD FIGHT

SHE FINISHED HER COURSE

SHE KEPT THE FAITH

NOW SHE GETS TO WEAR HER CROWN

A BROTHER LIKE MINE

TRIBUTE TO GYSGT USMC (RET) CHESTER "LEE" GILES

Jan 11, 1943-November 2, 2009

A BROTHER LIKE MINE

WAS FUN ALL THE TIME

A BROTHER LIKE MINE

WOULD GIVE YOU HIS LAST DIME

A BROTHER LIKE MINE

A GREAT HUSBAND, FATHER, GRANDFATHER AND FRIEND

A BROTHER LIKE MINE

WAS THERE NO MATTER WHEN

A BROTHER LIKE MINE

WOULD LEND A LISTENING EAR

HE PROVED AT THE END, THERE WAS NO FEAR

2 CORINTHAINS 5:8(KVJ)

WE ARE CONFIDENT I SAY AND WILLING RATHER TO BE ABSENT FROM THE FLESH AND TO BE PRESENT WITH THE LORD